STAR WARS

THE LAST JEDI

™

HEROES
OF THE GALAXY

Written by Ruth Amos

DK | Penguin
Random
House

Project Editor Ruth Amos
Designer Chris Gould
Senior Editor David Fentiman
Senior Designer Owen Bennett
Pre-production Producer Marc Staples
Senior Producer Mary Slater
Managing Editor Sadie Smith
Managing Art Editor Victoria Short
Publisher Julie Ferris
Art Director Lisa Lanzarini
Publishing Director Simon Beecroft

For Lucasfilm
Assistant Editor Samantha Holland
Art Director Troy Alders
Story Group James Waugh, Pablo Hidalgo,
and Leland Chee
Image Unit Steve Newman, Newell Todd,
Gabrielle Levenson, Erik Sanchez, and Bryce Pinkos
Photographers Jonathan Olley, Ed Miller, John Wilson,
Shannon Kirbie, David James, and Bruno Dayan

First American Edition, 2017
Published in the United States by DK Publishing
345 Hudson Street, New York, New York 10014

Page design copyright © 2017 Dorling Kindersley Limited
DK, a Division of Penguin Random House LLC
17 18 19 20 21 10 9 8 7 6 5 4 3 2 1
001–298133–Dec/2017

© & TM 2017 LUCASFILM LTD.

A catalog record for this book is available from the Library of Congress.

ISBN: 978-1-4654-5578-9 (Paperback)
ISBN: 978-1-4654-5579-6 (Hardcover)

DK books are available at special discounts when purchased in bulk for
sales promotions, premiums, fund-raising, or educational use. For details, contact:
DK Publishing Special Markets, 345 Hudson Street, New York, New York 10014
SpecialSales@dk.com

Printed and bound in China

A WORLD OF IDEAS:
SEE ALL THERE IS TO KNOW

www.dk.com
www.starwars.com

Contents

4   Meet the Resistance

6   Escape!

8   Resistance fleet

10   The chase is on!

12   Supreme Leader
        Snoke

14   General Leia
        Organa

16   Vice Admiral Holdo

18   Poe Dameron

20   Rose and Finn

22   Greedy guests

24   Canto Bight dos and don'ts

26   At the races

28   DJ

30   Luke Skywalker

32   Island tour

34   Rey

36   Kylo Ren

38   On board the *Supremacy*

40   Captain Phasma

42   General Hux

44   Quiz

46   Glossary

47   Index

Meet the Resistance

The galaxy is at war! The brave Resistance is battling the First Order. The First Order wants to rule the whole galaxy, but the Resistance fights back.

Admiral Ackbar

General Leia Organa

The Resistance has a secret
base on the planet D'Qar,
but the First Order discovers
where it is. The heroes must
escape quickly before the
First Order attacks the base.

Vice Admiral
Holdo

Lieutenant
Connix

Escape!

The Resistance tries to flee
the base in starships. Oh no!
Some First Order Star Destroyers
and a huge dreadnought ship
appear. The First Order will
use the dreadnought's cannons
to blast the Resistance.

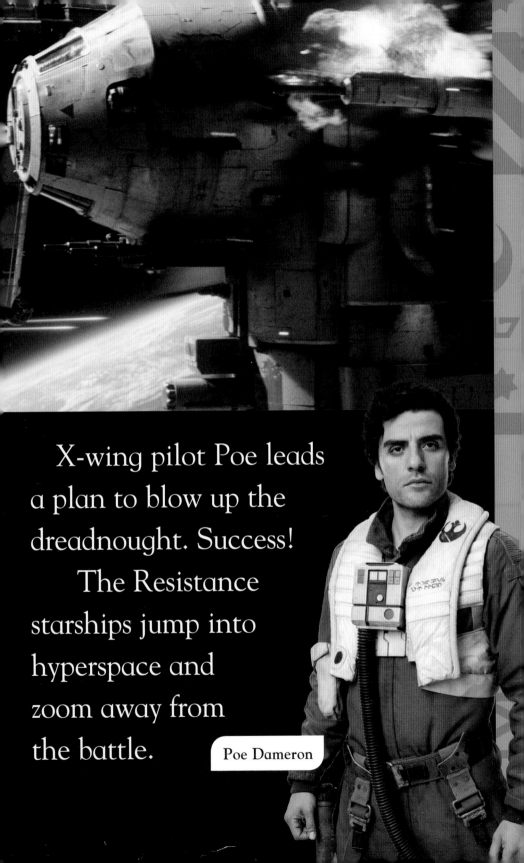

X-wing pilot Poe leads a plan to blow up the dreadnought. Success! The Resistance starships jump into hyperspace and zoom away from the battle.

Poe Dameron

RESISTANCE FLEET

The Resistance's starship fleet may be smaller than the First Order's, but it packs a punch!

Admiral Ackbar commands the fleet.

A-WING

Manufacturer: Kuat Systems Engineering

Weapons: Missiles, laser cannons

Strengths: Speedy, able to provide cover

Tallie Lintra pilots an A-wing.

X-WING

Manufacturer:
Incom-FreiTek

Weapons: Laser cannons, proton torpedos

Strengths: Versatile, nimble

C'ai Threnalli pilots an X-wing.

RESISTANCE BOMBER

Manufacturer:
Slayn and Korpil

Weapons: Proton bombs, tail guns

Strengths: Sturdy, great firepower

Paige Tico is a gunner on board a bomber.

The chase is on!

The First Order fleet is right behind the Resistance!
It followed the Resistance starships all the way through hyperspace.
Now it is chasing after them.

Captain Phasma

General Hux

General Hux leads the chase. He commands the First Order's huge fleet. It includes 30 Star Destroyers. Hux also commands thousands of stormtroopers and officers, with Captain Phasma's help.

First Order officer

First Order executioner

Supreme Leader Snoke

Who is the scary figure sitting
on a throne? It is Supreme Leader
Snoke. He is the ruler of the
First Order. His headquarters are
on a Mega-Destroyer warship.
Supreme Leader Snoke wants
total control of the galaxy.

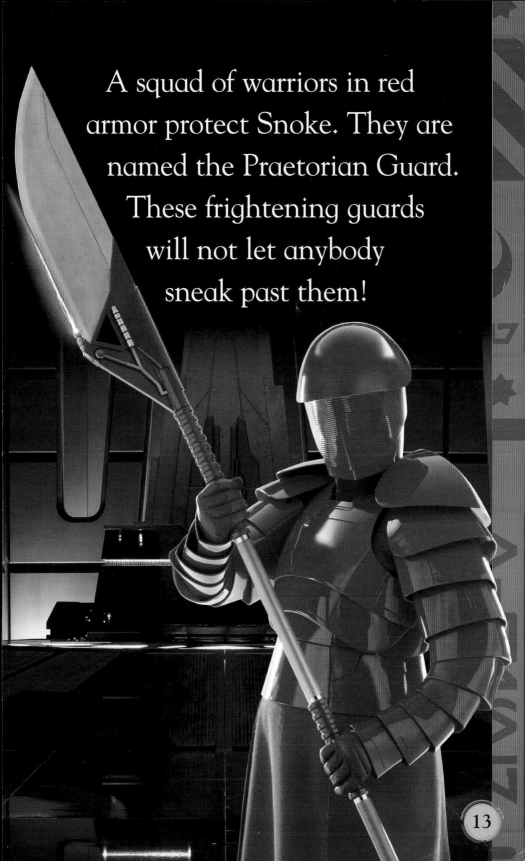

A squad of warriors in red
armor protect Snoke. They are
named the Praetorian Guard.
These frightening guards
will not let anybody
sneak past them!

General Leia Organa

General Leia is the founder of the Resistance. This wise leader makes important decisions. How can she bring her fleet to safety and defeat the First Order?

Leia commands her troops from the Resistance's largest starship, a cruiser. Unfortunately, the First Order damages the cruiser during the chase. Poor Leia is badly wounded.

Shiny droid C-3PO is Leia's advisor and friend.

Vice Admiral Holdo

When Leia is injured, Vice Admiral Amilyn Holdo becomes the leader of the Resistance.

The crew members listen to Holdo's speech.

Holdo must take control and
bring the fleet out of danger.

Holdo gives a speech to the
Resistance fighters. She tells them
that they must not give up hope.
It is very important for them
to keep fighting the First Order.

Poe Dameron

Amazing pilot Poe is not afraid
to put himself in danger.
But sometimes he is too reckless.
When Poe ignores Leia's orders,
she demotes him from the rank
of commander to captain!

Poe and his loyal droid BB-8 head into action.

Holdo does not trust Poe. She thinks he causes too much trouble. Poe does not trust Holdo either. He is worried that she does not have a good plan to escape the First Order.

Rose and Finn

Rose works in the Resistance ground crew. This talented technician repairs starfighters. She has hated the First Order ever since she was a child.

Finn is a determined Resistance fighter. He and Rose must try to find a codebreaker in Canto Bight city. The codebreaker can give them security codes. They will use the codes to sneak on board Snoke's Mega-Destroyer.

Greedy guests

These weird and wonderful aliens are visitors to Canto Bight's casinos. They are some of the richest and most important aliens in the galaxy!

The casino guests come from many different planets. They wear fancy, expensive clothes. These aliens are greedy criminals, who have made their fortunes in galactic wars.

CANTO BIGHT
DOs AND DON'Ts

DO celebrate when you're winning a game.

DO gobble down a brightly colored, delicious cake.

DO take a ride around the city in your shiny new speeder.

DON'T forget to admire the casinos' stained glass windows.

DON'T mistake BB-8 for a gaming machine.

DON'T cheat in the casinos. Canto Bight's police will arrest you!

DON'T stick to one type of gaming machine. Be sure to try them all!

At the races

The aliens of Canto Bight love to watch fathier racing. Fathiers are long-legged, elegant creatures. They can gallop very quickly. Jockeys wear bright outfits and helmets. They ride the fathiers around a race track.

Jockey

Fathier

Stable keeper

Stablehand girl

The stable keeper is a cruel,
bad-tempered alien. He does not
treat the fathiers well.
He is unkind to the children
who work in the stables, too.

DJ

Canto Bight police officers catch Rose and Finn and put them in jail. They share a cell with DJ, a thief and criminal.

DJ's name stands for "don't join." He does not want to join the First Order or the Resistance. He believes both sides are equally bad. But when Rose and Finn agree to pay him, sneaky DJ unlocks the cell door and they escape!

Luke Skywalker

Luke lives alone in a hut on the planet Ahch-To.

Luke was once a Jedi Master, who trained students to become Jedi. One of the students turned to the dark side and destroyed the others. Luke blames himself for this and feels guilty.

Now, Luke believes the Jedi Order should end! He thinks the Jedi have caused many of the problems in the galaxy.

ISLAND
TOUR

Take a trip to Luke's rocky, windswept home! There are lots of sights to discover...

Luke lives in a simple, round stone hut with small windows.

A group of aliens known as the Caretakers looks after the island's stone buildings.

Flocks of cute, bird-like creatures named porgs roost in the cliffs.

A large thala-siren rests on the rocks by the waves.

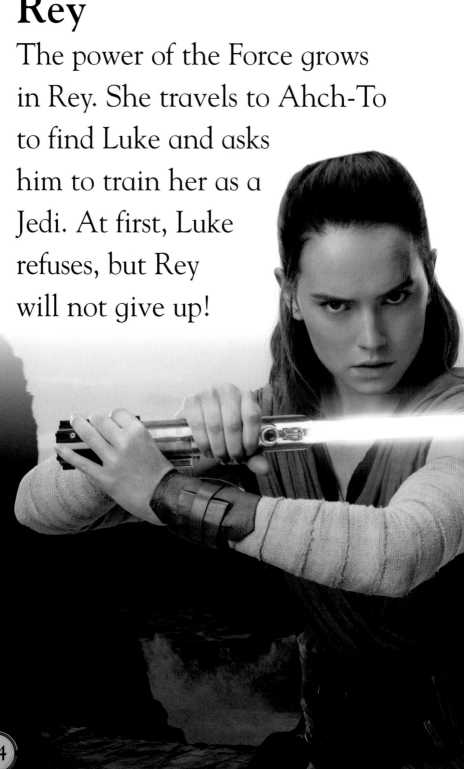

Rey

The power of the Force grows in Rey. She travels to Ahch-To to find Luke and asks him to train her as a Jedi. At first, Luke refuses, but Rey will not give up!

Eventually Luke agrees to
teach her how to use the Force
and fight with a lightsaber.
He tells Rey that the Force is
an energy. It connects every
living thing in the galaxy.

Kylo Ren

This First Order warrior is Snoke's apprentice. Kylo faced Rey in a lightsaber duel, but was defeated. Snoke is very disappointed in Kylo for his failure. Angry Kylo wants to prove himself to Snoke. He seeks revenge on both Rey and the Resistance!

Kylo pilots a special TIE silencer with spiky wings to chase after the Resistance fleet.

TIE silencer

ON BOARD THE *SUPREMACY*

THRONE ROOM

Snoke gives out orders from his throne. The throne room is deep inside the ship.

TRACKING ROOM

This room has special equipment. The First Order uses it to track the Resistance.

Snoke's Mega-Destroyer warship, the *Supremacy*, is his command center. The enormous *Supremacy* is the biggest ship in the First Order's fleet!

HANGAR
This big space holds TIE fighters and legions of stormtroopers.

CREW
The ship's crew includes many creepy BB droids and scary First Order officers.

Captain Phasma

Captain Phasma leads the First Order's army of stormtroopers. She makes sure her soldiers are on high alert for any sightings of the Resistance.

Phasma is determined to track down ex-stormtrooper Finn, who deserted the First Order.

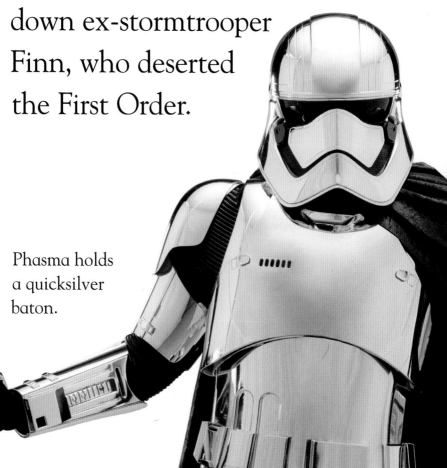

Phasma holds a quicksilver baton.

She discovers that Finn and Rose are on a secret mission on board the *Supremacy*. Phasma puts them both under arrest!

General Hux

General Hux is in charge
of the First Order's military.
When the Resistance fighters
escape from D'Qar, Snoke is furious
with Hux for failing to stop them.
Snoke orders Hux to hunt down
the Resistance fleet.

Hux is determined to wipe out
all the Resistance fighters.
He believes they are criminals.

Hux visits the
Supremacy
ship to receive
Snoke's orders.

Quiz

1. Which type of starfighter does Tallie pilot?

2. Who guards Supreme Leader Snoke and wears red armor?

3. Who becomes the leader of the Resistance after General Leia is injured?

4. Why does Leia demote Poe to a lower rank?

5. What type of racing do the aliens of Canto Bight love to watch?

6. What does DJ's name stand for?

7. Who looks after the stone buildings on Luke's island?

8. Which is the biggest starship in the First Order's fleet?

Answers on page 47

Glossary

apprentice
A student or pupil

demote
To give a person a lower rank or position

First Order
An evil group that seeks to rule the galaxy

fleet
A group of starships or vehicles that travel together

founder
A person who creates or starts up something

hyperspace
A method that starships use to travel
faster than light

Resistance
A group that defends the galaxy from the First Order

sturdy
Strongly built

versatile
Able to be used for many different purposes

Index

Ahch-To 30, 34

BB-8 19, 25

C-3PO 14

Canto Bight 20, 22, 24–25, 26, 28

Captain Phasma 10, 11, 40–41

Caretakers, the 32

criminals 23, 28, 42

D'Qar 5, 42

DJ 28–29

dreadnought 6, 7

fathiers 26–27

Finn 20, 28, 40, 41

First Order fleet 10–11, 39

General Hux 10, 11, 42–43

General Leia Organa 4, 14–15, 16, 18

Jedi 30, 34

Kylo Ren 36–37

lightsaber 35, 36

Luke Skywalker 30–31, 32, 34, 35

Poe Dameron 7, 18–19

porgs 33

Praetorian Guard 13

Resistance fleet 8–9, 10, 14, 17, 36, 42

Rey 34–35, 36

Rose 20, 28, 41

stormtroopers 11, 39, 40

Supremacy, the 38–39, 41, 42

Supreme Leader Snoke 12–13, 20, 36, 38, 39, 42

Vice Admiral Holdo 5, 16–17, 19

Answers to the quiz on pages 44 and 45:
1. A-wing 2. Praetorian Guard 3. Vice Admiral Holdo
4. Because Poe ignores Leia's orders. 5. Fathier racing
6. "Don't join" 7. The Caretakers 8. The *Supremacy*

A LEVEL FOR EVERY READER

This book is a part of an exciting four-level reading series to support children in developing the habit of reading widely for both pleasure and information. Each book is designed to develop a child's reading skills, fluency, grammar awareness, and comprehension in order to build confidence and enjoyment when reading.

Ready for a Level 2 (Beginning to Read) book

A child should:

- be able to recognize a bank of common words quickly and be able to blend sounds together to make some words.
- be familiar with using beginner letter sounds and context clues to figure out unfamiliar words.
- sometimes correct his/her reading if it doesn't look right or make sense.
- be aware of the need for a slight pause at commas and a longer one at periods.

A valuable and shared reading experience

For many children, reading requires much effort, but adult participation can make reading both fun and easier. Here are a few tips on how to use this book with a young reader:

Check out the contents together:

- read about the book on the back cover and talk about the contents page to help heighten interest and expectation.
- discuss new or difficult words.
- chat about labels, annotations, and pictures.

Support the reader:

- give the book to the young reader to turn the pages.
- where necessary, encourage longer words to be broken into syllables, sound out each one, and then flow the syllables together; ask him/her to reread the sentence to check the meaning.
- encourage the reader to vary her/his voice as she/he reads; demonstrate how to do this if helpful.

Talk at the end of each book, or after every few pages:

- ask questions about the text and the meaning of the words used—this helps develop comprehension skills.
- read the quiz at the end of the book and encourage the reader to answer the questions, if necessary, by turning back to the relevant pages to find the answers.